EARLY INDIAN ARCHITECTURE

CITIES AND CITY GATES ETC.

Early Indian Architecture

CITIES AND CITY GATES ETC.

ANANDA K. COOMARASWAMY

MANOHAR
2024

First published 1930
Reprinted 2024

ISBN 978-81-19139-63-7

Published by
Ajay Kumar Jain *for*
Manohar Publishers & Distributors
4753/23 Ansari Road, Daryaganj
New Delhi 110 002

Printed at
Replika Press Pvt. Ltd.

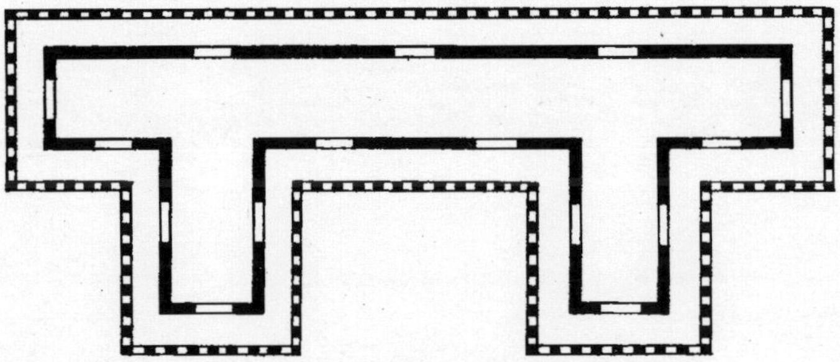

FIG. 1. UPPER STOREY (*uttamāgāra*)

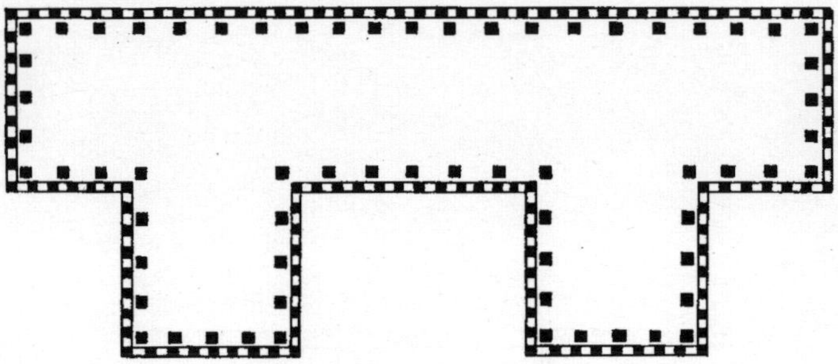

FIG. 2. SECOND STOREY (*ardhatala*)

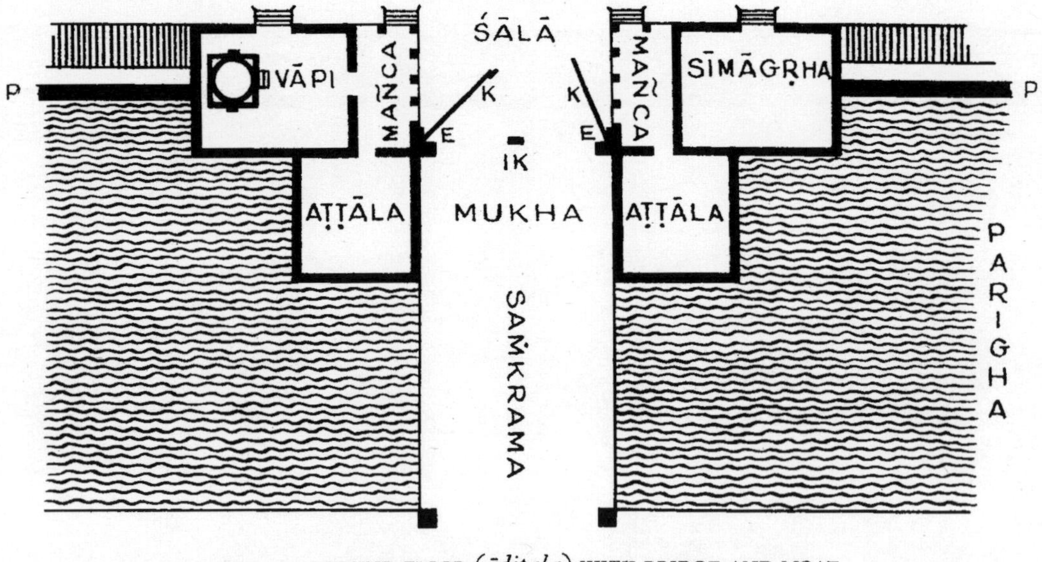

FIG. 3. GROUND FLOOR (*āditala*) WITH BRIDGE AND MOAT

Plans of a city gate (based on Kauṭilīya Arthaśāstra and early reliefs)

PLATE CXXII. *Coomaraswamy: Early Indian Architecture*

EARLY INDIAN ARCHITECTURE[1]

By ANANDA K. COOMARASWAMY

I. CITIES AND CITY-GATES, ETC.

The old Indian city is by no means to be regarded as a typically Brahmanical institution. Apart from the fact that we have remains of well-developed pre-Aryan cities in the Indus Valley sites,[2] and from the fact that the Vedas make occasional reference to the "cities of the Dasyus," it is to be observed that in the Brahmanical law books, which are very nearly, if not quite contemporary with the architectural period to be discussed below, cities are despised, and there are no ceremonies for urban life; the *Baudhāyana Dharma Sūtra*, II, 3, 6, 33, says "It is impossible for one to obtain salvation, who lives in a town covered with dust."

Flourishing cities nevertheless certainly existed in centuries preceding the Christian era. Megasthenes writing, about 300 B. C., described Pāṭaliputra as over nine miles in length. References to and descriptions of cities, and city organization in Buddhist literature, in KA., and in the Epics, and the representations in early Buddhist reliefs all suggest that in the Maurya period we have already to do, not with any new developments, but with the continuation of a long-established and familiar type of urban organization.

Some of the most detailed descriptions of cities are to be found in Mil. 1, 34, and 330 ff. The last of these, despite its length, may be quoted in full. "Just as the architect of a city, when he wants to build one, would first search out a pleasant spot of ground, with which no fault can be found, even, with no hills or gullies in it, free from rough ground, and rocks, not open to danger of attack. And then when he has made plain any rough places there may still be on it, he would clear it thoroughly of all stumps and stakes, and would proceed to build there a city fine and regular, measured out into quarters, with excavated moats and ramparts about it, with stout gate-houses and towers, with market-places, cross-roads, street-corners, and public squares, with cleanly and even main roads, with regular lines of open shops, well-provided with parks, gardens, lakes, lotus-ponds, and wells, adorned with many kinds of temples of the gods, free from every fault. And then, when the city stood there in all its glory, he would go away to some other land." There follows a long list of those who will inhabit such a city, nobles, soldiers, craftsmen, and of the foreigners who will resort to it: "all these coming to take up their residence there, and finding the new city to be regular, faultless, perfect, and pleasant, would know 'Able indeed must that architect have been by whom this city was built!' Just so . . . the Blessed One's City of Righteousness has righteousness for its rampart, and fear of sin for its moat, knowledge for its city-gate, zeal for the

[1]Mainly as referred to in the Pali literature and as represented in the reliefs of Bharhut, Sāñcī, and Amarāvatī. Terms are cited in Pali, Sanskrit, or Prakrit, according to their source. Where no particular text is cited, it is to be understood that the term is of very common occurrence, or that the sense is well known.

Abbreviations: Cull., *Cullavagga;* DhA., *Dhammapada Atthakathā;* DHA, Acharya, *Dictionary of Hindu architecture;* Div., *Divyāvadāna;* DN., *Dīgha Nikāya;* IAT., my *Indian architectural terms*, JAOS, vol. 48, 1928; J., *Jātaka* (Fausböll); KA., *Kauṭilīya Arthaṣāstra* (Bk II, Ch. 21 unless otherwise stated); Mhv., *Mahāvaṁsa;* Mv., *Mahāvagga;* Mil., *Milindapañha*; MN., *Majjhima Nikāya;* MSA., my *Mediæval Sinhalese art;* PvA., *Pethavatthu Atthakathā;* SBE., *Sacred Books of the East*

The *vaḍḍhakī, vaḍḍhakī* (Skt. *vardhakī*), architect, builder, carpenter (also shipwright, J. VI, 432), is by far the most important and oftenest mentioned of the craftsmen. Cf. Miln. 345. "When men see a pleasant city, they know by inference how great the *vaḍḍhakī* was." In J. II, 208, we have a Brāhmaṇavaḍḍhakī. Tools used by *vaḍḍhakīs* include adzes (*vāsi*, J. II, 18 and IV, 344); chisels (*nikhādana*, J. IV, 344), hammers (*muggara*, ib.), measuring line (*sutta, kāla sutta*, J. IV, 344 and VI, 332, pegged out with wooden pegs, *khāṇuka*, J. VI, 332); they work *sippānurūpena* "according to *silpa*-plans," perhaps a reference to *śilpa-śastras* (cf. *sippa, sippavant* in Pali Dictionaries). DHA rendering of *vardhakī* as "painter" is absurd. In Mhv. LXXXVIII, 106, 107, *itthikā-, cuṇṇa-, dāru-* and *silā-vaḍḍhakīs* are mentioned, i.e., bricklayers, plasterers, timberers (carpenters) and masons. While *vaḍḍhakī*, alone, is the carpenter as architect, we also get *tacchaka* as woodworker, Mil. 413.

[2]"The true creators of the city state were the Sumerians . . . the higher city civilisations of the Old World from the Mediterranean to India do form a great unity, and it seems possible to affirm their fundamental community alike in type and origin," Dawson, *The age of the gods*, pp. 117, 118. In other words, the city in Indian culture belongs to the "Early Asiatic" inheritance, and certainly cannot be regarded either as characteristically Aryan, or as a recent development in Maurya times.

FIG. 4. CITY OF KAPILAVATTHU

FIG. 5. CITY OF JETUTTARA (*Vessantara Jātaka*)

FIG. 6. CITY OF KUSINĀRĀ (WAR OF THE RELICS)

City gates, from Sāñcī

PLATE CXXIII. *Coomaraswamy: Early Indian Architecture*

gate-tower, faith for the pillars at its base, mindfulness for the guard, and wisdom for the palace, the Suttantas for the market place, the Abhidhamma for the public square, the Vinaya for its judgment hall, and constant self-possession for its street."[3]

Let us now assemble the available data in a more systematic way. Cities (*nagara*, *pura*) are built by city or master architects (*nagara-vaḍḍhakī*, *mahā-°*, Mil. 1, 2, 330; J. VI, 332), assisted by other carpenters (*vaḍḍhakī*, J. II, 18; IV, 153, 344; VI, 4, 27, etc.) and bricklayers (*iṭṭhaka-vaḍḍhakī*, Mhv. XXX, 5; J. VI, 333). All these live in villages, and are summoned when work is to be done. Of the carpenters in particular we learn that they lived in villages of their own, going up river to cut and fetch timber for town houses (J. II, 18; VI, 427). Eighteen guilds of craftsmen are employed in building a new city, and amongst these guilds (*seṇi*) are cited the aforesaid carpenters, the superior smiths (*kammāra*), workmen (*cammakāra*),[4] decorators and painters (*cittakāra*), "and others skilled in various crafts (*sippa*)" (J. VI, 427, cf. list of craftsmen in Mil. 331), who work according to the traditions of their craft (*sippānurūpena*, J. VI, 332).

The most conspicuous and necessary parts of a city are the moat (*pārikhā*) and rampart (*pākāra*), gates (*dvāra*, *gopura*), more specifically gate-houses (*dvāra-koṭṭhaka*), with their defense towers (*dvāra-aṭṭālaka*, *gopura-°*), other defense towers within and near, but not upon the rampart (*antaraṭṭāla*, J. II, 400), and the king's palace (*pāsāda*, *harmya*, *rāja-nivesana*, *vimāna*, etc.). Then there are other mansions (*nivesana*, *kūṭāgāra*) and houses (*geha*), temples (*devaṭṭhāna*, Mil. 92, 330; *koṣṭhaka*, a temple granary, KA., Ch. 25), granaries (*koṭṭha*, *koṭṭhaka*), resthouses or sarais (*sālā*, *puṇya-sālā*, J. I, 200 = *vissamana-sālā*, DhA. I, 269/270), halls and arenas for sport (*kīḷa-sālā*, *kīḷa-maṇḍala*, J. VI, 332/333 monasteries (*paṇṇa-sālā*), almonries (*dāna-sālā*, at city and palace gates, J. I, 262, IV, 402, VI, 97, 484, 487; *dānagga* "in hundreds," Mil. 2) elephant stables (*hatthi-sālā* J. VI, 432, etc.), shops (*āpaṇa*), bazaars (*antarāpaṇa*, Mil. 2), saloons, cook-shops, taverns, slaughterhouses (*pānāgara*, *odaniyā-ghara*, *soṇḍā*, *suṇā*, J. VI, 276, etc.).

There are parks (*uyyāna*, Mil. 34; J. III, 238, VI, 333), gardens (*ārāma*, Mil. 34) and flower-gardens (*pupphārāma*, DhA. I, 270), lotus ponds and bathing tanks (*pokkharinī*, *nāhana-pokkharinī*, *nāhanodaka*, *udapāna*, *taḷāka*); sacred trees (*rukkha-cetiya*, often at the gates). There are main streets (*rāja-magga*, *mahā-patha*, *torana-magga*, J. I, 199/200, III, 217, etc.), ordinary streets (*vīthi*, J. I, 89, and *antaravīthi*, J. I, 340), alleys and blind lanes (*patatthi*, *sandhi-bbūha*, J. III, 217), a main public square (*singhāṭaka*, Mil. 62; J. VI, 276), a market place (*caccara*, Mil. 332, meaning rather dubious), other squares and street crossings (*cattuka*, Mil. 34; J. I, 326 and 340; *sandhi*, Mil. 330). That some streets at least were exclusively inhabited by members of particular trades or castes, as in modern Indian cities, is indicated by J. VI, 485, *vessānaṁ vīthiyā*, *vessa-vithiyā*, "street of the Vaiśyas or merchants." Evidently the four main streets (*catumahāpatha*, J. I, 199/200) led direct from the gates to the central square (*singhāṭaka*) on which the palace abutted; for a city elder from the *singhāṭaka* can see a man coming from East, South, West or North (Mil. 62); a man proceeds directly from the city gate to the palace (J. VI, 412); and the *catumahāpathe*, as the place where a sarai is built (J. I, 200/201) is clearly equivalent to *singhāṭake*. A drain or sewer (*niddhamana*, *niddhamana-magga*, J. I, 425, 490) leads out of the city, and it is possible for a man to make his escape by it. Outside the city are suburbs (*nigama*, J. VI, 330), and rural villages (*yava-majjhaka-gāma*, J. VI, 330).

The city is laid out in quarters, *bhāgaso mitaṁ*, Mil. 1, J. VI, 46, etc. The plan is rectangular, usually square, with four gates, one in the middle of each wall, facing

[3]Based on the translation in SBE XXXVI, with verbal changes.

[4]*Cammakāra*, "leather-workers," but often apparently equivalent to *rathakāra*, wright or artisan generally, e.g., J. V, 174; PvA. 175. If *cammakāra*, as is not improbable, is equivalent to blacksmith or ironworker, this would be with reference to the use of leather bellows, cf. MSA., p. 194.

In J. VI, 432, sappers using leather sacks (*cammāluka*) dig earth and build ramparts; but the *cammakāra* are evidently craftsmen, not coolies.

FIG. 7. FROM AN ARCHITRAVE, MATHURĀ (CAT. I, 38)

FIG. 8. CITY OF KUSINĀRĀ
(WAR OF THE RELICS)

FIG. 9. CITY OF JETUTTARA
(*Vessantara Jātaka*)

FIG. 10. CITY OF KOSALA

FIG. 11. CITY OF RĀJAGAHA

City gates, from Mathurā (Fig. 7) and Sāñcī (Figs. 8–11)

PLATE CXXIV. *Coomaraswamy: Early Indian Architecture*

the four quarters (J. I, 262; II, 171, 194; III, 129; IV, 83, 425; VI, 330, 347),[5] and as we have seen, four main streets led from these gates to the centre of the city. The gates are closed at night or in time of war (J. II, 412; VI, 406), and opened in the morning in time of peace. In the most general way the gates are called *dvāra*, or less often *gopura* (J. VI, 276, has the gloss *dvāra* = *gopura*); but more specifically, the term gate-house (*dvāra-koṭṭhaka*) is constantly employed. As the city is approached from without, the gate-house (also called *daḷha-gopura*, *daḷham-aṭṭāla-koṭṭha*, *daḷha-gopura-aṭṭāla-koṭṭha*) came into view, with its defense towers (*dvāra-aṭṭālaka*, *gopura-aṭṭālaka*)[6] on the city side of the moat.

The city is always surrounded by a moat or moats (*parikhā*, Skt. *paligha*) or at least a dry ditch. In the reliefs, the moat is indicated by growing lotuses, and in many cases the actual water is also shown; occasionally we see women from the city going down to the moat to fetch water, and in one case there is access on the city side through a little gate, so that the moat on the city side becomes effectively a *ghāṭ* (Fig. 4). In the texts, the water is usually taken for granted, but in J. VI, 432, a water-moat, *udaka-parikhā*, is specified. In Mil. I, the moat is "deep," *gambhīra*. In Mhv. XXV, 48, we find reference to a great triple moat, *timahāparikhā*; and the gloss to *utkiṇṇantara-parikhaṁ*, "deep excavated inner moat" of J. IV, 106, defines three successive external moats, *udaka-*, *kaddama-* and *sukha-parikhā*, one within the other, respectively a water moat, a mud moat, and a pleasure moat. J. VI, 276, has *parikhāyo*, moats, in the plural.

On the city side of the moat rises the wall (*pākāra*, Skt. *prākāra*), from a foundation or plinth (*vapra*)[7], which in the case of a dry ditch should perhaps be called a glacis. It is generally indicated in the reliefs that city walls are made of brick, but in one Sāñcī relief (Figs. A and 4), we find what is evidently a wooden wall of palisade construction,[8] and in this case the wall is continued along the edge of the bridge leading to the gateway; the *Uttarādhyayana Sūtra*, 30, 16 is authority for a *paṁśuprākāra*, earthen (laterite) wall, of a city. Mil. 1 has *paṇḍara-pākāra*, white wall.

Sometimes the wall is shown with reëntrant angles. It is finished off at the top either by a coping or more usually by battlements. In no case (single exception, Fig. 16), are towers on the walls represented, nor have I found any reference in the texts to the existence of such towers; defense towers are either the regular *dvāraṭṭāla* of the gate-houses, or free-standing towers (*antaraṭṭāla*) near the walls but within them (Figs. B, 6, 8, 11, etc.). The walls could be manned, having, no doubt, an inner gallery or pathway a little below the top, and approached by stairs as suggested in the plan (Fig. 3). The top (*matthaka*) of the wall was of some width: in J. VI, 275, Puṇṇaka's horse gallops along the *pākāra matthaka*.

The gate-house was approached by a bridge (*saṅkama*, Mil. 92, *saṁkrama*, KA) in the case of a water-moat, or earthen causeway (*pūrdvāri mṛtkūṭa*, *Śiśupālavadha*, III, 68, gloss) when the city was defended only by a dry ditch. Such a bridge or causeway seems to have been designated by the curious name of "elephant's nail" (*hastinakha*).[9] Such bridges, like thoroughfares, are public places, unsuited for serious talk (Mil. 92).

The traveller, crossing the bridge, and entering the city, passes between two

[5]But one Sāñcī relief (Fig. 6) shows two gates (one of unique form), not far apart in a single line of wall. Obviously, large cities must have had more than four gates; Pāṭaliputra, according to Megasthenes, had sixty-four. In Mhv. LXXXVIII, 116, the wall of Pulatthipura is circular: cf. representations of Ujjain in Jāina MSS., e.g. *Cat. Indian Collections, Boston*, Pt. IV, Pl. X (folio 75).

[6]In the *Uttarādhyayana Sūtra*, *ṭīkā*, IX, 18 (Charpentier, p. 314), gloss on *gopuraṭṭāla*, we have "the towers are military structures (*āyodhasthānāni*) connected with the rampart-house (*prākārakoṣṭha*, presumably = *dvārakoṭṭhaka*).

[7]*Vapra* may be sometimes synonymous with *pākāra* (DHA, 534), but in KA XXIV we have *vaprasyopari prākāram*.

[8]Doubtless heavy planks laid horizontally and fastened by solid uprights. This type of construction is well seen in the conduit (*niddhamana?*) walls recently excavated at Pāṭaliputra (*Illustrated London News*, March 24, 1928, p. 477).

[9]"Elephant's nail," originally a kind of capital composed of addorsed elephants, their forefeet projecting beyond the abacus so as to make the toe-nails conspicuous when seen from below; secondly, a balcony or bridge supported by such a capital; finally, even a causeway substituted for such a bridge. See IAT, pp. 258, 259. (It was by an oversight (thinking of *kesara-nakha*) that I adduced *kesa-nakha* (which means hair and nail-paring relics) as a parallel here).

FIG. 12. CITY OF RĀJAGAHA(?)

FIG. 13. CITY OF BENARES
(*Chaddanta Jātaka*)

FIG. 14

FIG. 15. CITY OF KUSINĀRĀ
(PARTITION OF THE RELICS)

FIG. 16

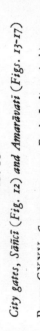

FIG. 17

City gates, Sāñcī (Fig. 12) and Amarāvatī (Figs. 13-17)

PLATE CXXV. *Coomaraswamy: Early Indian Architecture*

high towers, the *dvāra-aṭṭālaka*, *gopura-aṭṭālaka*; these are forwardly projecting members of the gate-house, towers of defense, to be manned in case of necessity (J. II, 217, and VI, 409, and as represented in the reliefs). In J. II, 244/5 we read of a king who ascends (*abhirūhitvā*) and again comes down from (*otaritvā*) a gate-tower; in all probability these towers contained the stairways which led to the upper floors (KA, Ch. 21, discussed below).

The main part of the gate-house is even or continuous (*prākāra-sama*, KA, and as seen in the reliefs), with the rampart on either side, and in the centre bridges the great hall (*sālā*) of the gate-house, and connects the two towers already mentioned; the two ends contiguous with the rampart extending to right and left of the forwardly projecting towers are similar to these in appearance, and form, in fact, two other towers of defence. The space between the projecting towers and immediately in front of the great gate-hall is the "mouth" (*mukha*,[10] KA, Ch. 21).

It is often clearly indicated in the reliefs that the whole basement of the gate-house is of brick. In any case, the basement wall is unbroken up to the level of the second storey, except that high up on the front face of each of the forward towers there is a small horizontal slit window; or more rarely a group of small square apertures; these loopholes probably served the double purpose of lighting the stairway inside, and of a post for archers. The ends of the supporting beams of the second or mezzanine floor (*ardha-tala*, KA) are generally clearly shown, projecting at the top of the basement wall. Probably with reference to its pavilion-like construction (*sthūṇāvabandha*, KA, Ch. 21) this second floor is designated *harmya* (*ib.*); a railing (*vedikā*), pillars (*thambha*) and cornice are always clearly shown. Above this is a top floor, supporting an attic-house or roof apartment (*uttamāgāra*, KA, Ch. 21), with brick walls, four gable window ends (*mahāvatapāna*) and thatched, barrel-vaulted roof (*chadana*), having its ridge (*kūṭa*), surmounted by finials (*ghaṭa* or *kalasa*, DhA, I, 414) on each gable and at intervals along the roof ridge. No doubt the barrel-vaulted roof was constructed as usual of curved rafters (*gopānasiyo*) resting against an internal roof-ridge (*kūṭa*, Mil. 38; DhA, I, 414), or if with apsidal ends, against circular or semi-circular roof plates (*kaṇṇikā*).[11] In J. VI, 125, the gateway of the Tāvatiṁsa heaven is called *citta-kūṭa-dvāra-koṭṭhaka* "gate-house of the painted (or decorated) roof-ridge." The same gate-house is set about with statues of Indra "as though guarded by tigers;" evidence, perhaps, that statues of a reigning king might be set up at a city gate.

The actual gateway, opened or closed as occasion required, consisted of a pair of heavy wooden panels (*kavāṭa*, Skt. *kapāṭa*), sometimes iron-bound or studded (*ayo-kammata-dvāra*, Mhv. XXV, 28) and turning on tenons above and below. The upper parts of these leaves closed against the top of the archway, (*toraṇaśiraḥ*, KA), the lower part against the heavy *indakhīla* (Skt. *indrakīla*) embedded in the ground between the pillars of the *toraṇa*, and forming a low threshold.[12] The gate leaves are not often visible in the reliefs, but can be very clearly seen in Figs. A and 4 where a half-opened leaf partly conceals a soldier standing in the entrance; and in Figs. C and 6 we see the besiegers battering on the leaves of the door (cf. *kavāṭe thāpetvā*, "beat against the door panels", in this case, however, of a palace, J. IV, 182). Having regard to the necessity of providing passage for elephants with riders, we may suppose the dimensions of the gate aperture to have been something like twenty by eighteen feet, and many existing mediæval city or fort gateways are quite as large as this; and from this, some idea of the size of the whole gate-house can be deduced.

[10]*Mukha*=entrance, not as structure, but as space: cf. the *bahimukha*, entrance from without, of apartments (*thāna*) in a sarai (*sālā*), J. VI, 333.

[11]See my *Pali kaṇṇikā=circular roof-plate*, to appear in J.A.O.S., vol 50.

[12]*Indakhīla*, in DhA, II, 180, 181, a symbol of stability. Generally, "threshold," e.g., Div. 250, 20; 365, I: *Mahāvastu*, I, 195, 16; I, 235, 12; I, 308, 7: *Madhyamikasūtravṛtti*, 199, 13. In J. I, 89, *indakhīle thito* "standing at the gate" (of Kapilavatthu). In DN. II, 254, we have *chetvā khilam* (v. l. *khīlam*) *chetvā paligham inda-khīlam ūhacca-m-anejā* "all bars and bolts are hewn in twain, the threshold-stone dug up." Professor Clark informs me that *indakhīla* is rendered in Tibetan (e.g. *Mahāvyutpatti*, ed. Sakaki, 5582) by words meaning "threshold" or "steps at the threshold." *Khīla* alone = pillar (DN. II, 254), and *kīla* has this sense when *indrakīla* denotes "Indra's flagstaff" as in *Mahābhārata*, VI, 59, 122.

FIG. 18. JAIPUR, CITY GATE (AFTER REUTHER)

FIG. 19. BĪJĀPUR, FORTRESS GATE (AFTER REUTHER)

Later city and fortress gates.

PLATE CXXVI. *Coomaraswamy: Early Indian Architecture*

The gate-leaves are framed at the sides by heavy jambs, usually called *esikā* (Mil. 332; J. II, 94/95 and VI, 276, glossed as *thambhas* set firmly in the ground) but the word *esikā* may include all the gateway pillars, that is the bolt post, jamb, and *toraṇa*-upright at each side (cf. Fig. 20). In J. VI, 276, *toraṇāni* is glossed *piṭṭha-saṁghāṭa* (the usual terms for jamb in the case of smaller doorways) but this must be regarded as a rather casual use of terms, not strictly correct: for the use of *toraṇāni* in the plural cf. Fig. 20. When closed, the gate-leaves are secured by one, or perhaps usually two (KA) heavy cross-bars (Pali *paligha*, Skt. *parigha*)[13] resting in slots in the bolt-posts immediately behind the jambs, for example *Buddhacarita*, V, 82, *guru-parigha-kapāṭa saṁvṛttā*, "the heavy bar and gate-leaves being closed." We also find mention of *aggalāni*, bolts, which are well known in connection with smaller doors; in J. VI, 276 and 483 the Commentator makes *aggalāni=dvāra-kavāṭāni*, but this again must be regarded as casual. In KA the fastenings of the *aṇidvāra* are called *hasti-parigha*. J. VI, 483 gives us *citraggala*, decorated bolt, and J. V, 169, *rajataggala*, silver bolt. When the gate is attacked by elephants, stress is laid on breaking down the *toraṇa* or *toraṇas*, breaking the *paligha*, and uprooting the *esikāni* (J. II, 94/95; DN. III; 14, 254).

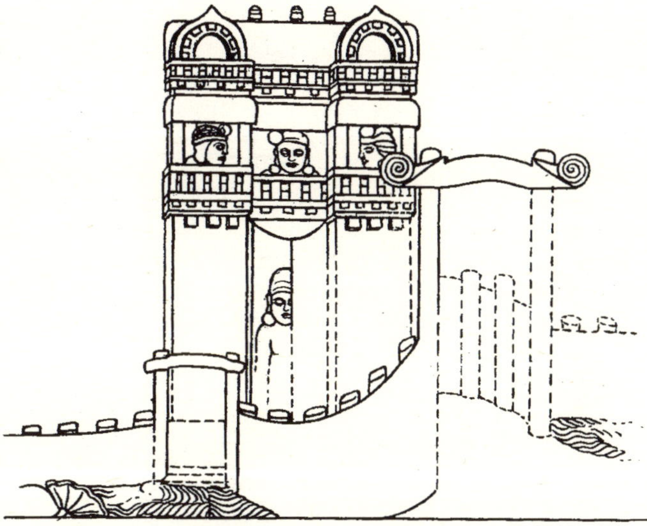

FIG. A. DIAGRAMMATIC SKETCH OF A GATE-HOUSE, MOAT, AND BRIDGE (SEE FIG. 4)

FIG. B. GATE-HOUSE, AND BUILDINGS WITHIN THE CITY-WALL. THE STRUCTURE IN FRONT TO RIGHT IS A MOVABLE VEHICLE, A KIND OF PALANKEEN. AMARĀVATĪ, MADRAS MUSEUM

Passing between the gate-posts (*esikāni*) under the arch (*toraṇa*) of the door, and between the two swinging door panels (*kavāṭa*) or when the great gates are closed, through the *cūḷa-* or *aṇidvāra* which opens through one of the large panels (J. VI, 391, 399, 401, and KA),[14] the traveller enters

[13]Pali *paligha* (=Skt. *parigha*) or *palikha* is always a cross-bar closing a gate, *parigha* (Skt. *paligha*) or *parikha* a moat. In J. II, 400, *parikhaṁ bhinditvā*, the sense requires *palikhaṁ*, and perhaps an emendation should be made.

[14]A smaller door cut in one of the large gate-leaves is a constant feature of mediæval gateways, and I have seen many examples. In J. VI, 406, the *cūḷa-dvāra* and *dvāra* (here= *kavāṭe*) of a city gate are contrasted; but *cūḷa-dvāra* is not exclusively a technical term for a door in a great gate, for in J. VI, 432, 460, *cūḷa* and *mahā-dvāras* are simply small and large doors of interior chambers. In the *Gobhila Gṛhya Sūtra*, IV, 7, 19–20 *aṇidvāra* is the back door of a house.

FIG. 20. CITY GATE DABHOI, GUJARĀT

FIG. 21. FORTRESS GATE, GWĀLIAR

Later city and fortress gates.

PLATE CXXVII. *Coomaraswamy: Early Indian Architecture*

a large hall (*sālā*, KA, Ch. 21) roofed by the second storey (*ardha-tala*) of the actual gate-house. On either side of him are stone platforms (*pratimañcau*).

An integral part of the gate-house is the *toraṇa* (*varaparava gopura-toraṇa*, "splendid gate-arch," Mil. 1), or arch against which the gate-leaves close from within; the upper part of this arch being designated *toraṇa-sirahs* (KA) and the threshold *inda-khīla*, Skt. *indrakīla* (see above). Such arches are easily recognizable in mediaeval fortress gates, e.g. at Dabhoi, Fig. 20, and Gwālior, Fig. 21, but they cannot be made out at Sāñcī or Amarāvatī, where we can hardly ever see far enough into the *mukha* for the actual gateway to be visible. In one case, at Sāñcī (Figs. A and 4) there is evidently no such arch, but there is a kind of semi-circular door-stop at the top. At Bharhut, no representation of a city gate is preserved, but we have several illustrations of *dvāra-koṭṭhakas* of palace or temple enclosures (Cunningham, *Bharhut*, Pls. XVIII, XIX); these are of a simpler type, but large enough to admit an elephant and rider, and here a pointed arch of the kind elsewhere so familiar in the early art, is a conspicuous feature of the structure.

I cannot satisfactorily explain the "high *patthaṇḍilā*" with which a city *gopura* is provided, Mhv., LX, 3; the upper stories (cf. *tala* in KA) of the gate-house may be meant. Cf. Geiger, *Cuḷavaṁsa*, trans. 1, 214; and MN, II, 155.

Quite distinct from the *toraṇa* of the actual gateway are the freestanding *toraṇas* which are frequently represented as situated at the bridge-end remote from the city; through these arches one must pass when entering or leaving the city, but it is obvious that they served an ornamental and honorific purpose, and had no value for defense. In function they differ in no way from the *toraṇas* elsewhere represented, or extant as at Sāñcī, as set up at the entrance to any sacred or honorable area or enclosure; and no doubt because they are taken for granted in this sense, and because they have no defensive value, we do not find them referred to in the literature.

FIG. C. A SECOND TYPE OF CITY-GATE, REPRESENTED ONLY IN ONE RELIEF (SEE FIG. 6). SĀÑCĪ

KA describes the gate-house of a fort (*durga*), substantially identical with that of a fortified city (for *durga-nagara* cf. *Āghāṭa-durgge* in the colophon of a Jāina manuscript described on p. 237); the nomenclature has already been made use of above. The passage is full of difficulties; but as these can be, at least in part, resolved by comparison with the passages cited already, it will be desirable to offer here a new rendering of the greater part of it.

The text informs us that "the ground floor (*āditala*) has five divisions, a hall (*śālā*), well-room (*vāpī*), and boundary-house (*sīmāgṛha*), and two platforms (*mañcau*) opposite to each other and each a tenth part of the whole (area)." I take this to refer to the ground plan thought of as of the lower part of the main structure as seen from the city side, and represented in the accompanying diagram, Plate 1 (based on KA, the Pali texts, and the reliefs).

FIG. 22. BODHI-GHARA, BHARHUT

PLATE CXXVIII. *Coomaraswamy: Early Indian Architecture*

Here the "hall" is the large passageway through the gate-house, i.e., the covered space, on the city side of the gate-leaves, appropriately called a hall because it is roofed by the superstructure. The "platforms" are clearly the open rooms with floors at some height above the road level, right and left of the hall; such platforms occur in all mediæval and later city gates, and are really the guard-rooms occupied by the soldiers (*dovārika*) on duty. Then the outermost room on one side is the well-room, that on the other, the "boundary-house," *sīmāgṛha*, explained by the Commentator as *koṣṭhagṛha*. Now in J. II, 378, we find the *doṇamāpaka*, the receiver of the king's dues paid in rice, seated at the door of the *koṭṭhāgāra*, superintending the measuring of the king's rice which has been brought into the city. Presumably, the granary door (*koṭṭhaka-dvāra*) is closed: anyhow, when it comes on to rain, the officer runs into the *dvāra-koṭṭhaka*, i. e., probably into the open *śālā*.[15] "Boundary-house" and "storehouse" are thus both designations of that part of the gate-house used for the temporary storage of taxes paid in kind; and possibly these should also be identified with the *sulka-śālā* or toll-house which, as we know, existed at the city gate for the collection of octroi on goods brought into the city for sale.

The text continues: "Then there is a pillared (*sthūnāvabandha*) pavilion (*harmya*) forming an elevated mezzanine floor (*ardhatala*) i.e., the second floor)." This is quite clear and corresponds exactly with many of the reliefs, e.g., Fig. 8, though the number of upper storeys may actually be one, two (as in KA), or three (cf. Fig. 9).

"Then there is an uppermost house (*uttamāgāra*) covering half the area (*vāstu*), or (in other words about) three-quarters the width (of the roof of the second story); this house has brick walls."

Here, too, the description suits the representations; and, generally speaking, nothing is commoner than such a roof-apartment, occupying the greater part of the flat roof of a building, but having a verandah space separating its walls from the railed parapet of the roof. The word *uttamāgāra* aptly describes such a roof-apartment.

"In the left (tower) there is a stairway turning rightwise, and in the other (tower) a stairway with concealed (or concealing) walls (*guḍhābhitti*)."

"The head (*sira*) of the gateway arch (*toraṇa*) measures two cubits. The two gate-panels (*kavāṭa*) occupy three-fifths (of the total width of the passage); there are two cross-bars (*parigha*) and an *indrakīla* of an ell's measure." The *indrakīla* is glossed as *kavāṭadhāranārtha pradāna*, and plausibly explained by Meyer as a kind of door-stop against which the folding panels meet below when they are closed.

"The accessory door (*aṇidvāra*) is five cubits in width and has four elephant cross-bars (*hasti-parigha*)." The position of the *aṇidvāra* and the exact significance of *hasti-parigha* are not clear; but perhaps what is meant is the small door generally to be found in one of the door panels, for use when the panels themselves are closed. Such a small square door might very well be said to have four *parighas* if we suppose the fastening to have been of the type illustrated in MSA., Fig. 82 (*daṇḍu-agula*).

"And for access an 'elephant's claw' (*hasti-nakha*) supporting a bridge (*saṁkrama*) level with the entrance (*mukha*); or an earthen embankment when there is no water (available for a moat)." I have shown elsewhere (IAT, pp. 258/259) that *hasti-nakha* is primarily a pillar with an elephant capital, and so-called because only the nails of the elephant's feet are visible to the observer from below. From the text above it is evident that the bridge over a moat was supported by such a pillar, and so perhaps in a derivative sense came also to be designated as a *hasti-nakha*; certainly Amara's gloss on *hasti-nakha* in *Śiśupālavadha*, III, 68, viz. *pūrdvāri mṛtkūṭaḥ*, shows that the

[15]For the use of the gate-hall in such a way, cf. J. VI, 514, where "the Bodhisattva did not enter the city, but sat down in the gate-hall (*nagara-dvāre nisīdi*):" and *Mṛcchakaṭikā*, III, 3, where a servant takes a nap in the *bahidvāra-sālā* (of the palace). For this typical use of gates in the East see Perrot et Chipiez, *La Perse*, II, pp. 69-72.

term had by his time come to denote the earthen embankment which formed a way down from the city gate to the open country beyond the ditch.

Finally, we have: "The gate-house (*gopura*) is to be made (accordingly), continuous with the rampart (*prākārasamam*), and built over the entrance (*mukhamavasthāpya*), and three parts of it form the 'lizard's mouth' (*godhāmukha*)." The last term presumably refers to the entrance itself, elsewhere simply called *mukha;* probably this "mouth" was also called "the lizard's mouth," just as we might call the gateway of a fortress "the lion's jaws": or *mukha* may apply to both the front and rear portions of the entrance.

Finally, it may be remarked that mediæval and even modern Indian architectural forms are directly derived from and often preserve the most characteristic features of the ancient forms. Some acquaintance, indeed, with a mediæval Indian fortress gateway is essential to a proper understanding of the description given in KA and discussed above; if, for example, one has passed through the iron-studded doors of a city or fortress gate-house still in use, or if the latter are closed, through the accessory door cut through one of the *kavāṭa* and noticed the guards seated on stone platforms (*cābutra*) right and left of the passage through the great hallway, the sense of the words *aṇidvāra* and *pratimañcau* becomes immediately evident. Or, as in Fig. 21, we may note how closely the whole construction of a modern gate-house may correspond to that represented in the ancient reliefs. I have not attempted to discuss the relationship of Indian city fortifications with Babylonian types, though analogies are evident (cf. the Ishtar gate of Babylon, Koldewey, *Das Ištartor*, Wiss D. O. G., No. 19, 1918).

Other articles in the present series will deal with tree temples (No. II of the series, printed below); houses and palaces; hermits' huts and domed shrines and early towers; windows, arches, and doorways; and pillars.

Description of the Illustrations

Plate I. Plans of a *dvāra-koṭṭhaka*, compiled from data cited in the text and from the reliefs; not to scale.

Fig. 1. *Uttamāgāra*. Fig. 2. *Ardhatala*. Fig. 3. *Āditala*. E = *esikānī:* IK = *indrakīla:* K = *kavāṭa:* P = *pākāra*. Thick black lines represent brick walls; small squares, pillars. The two pillars at the outer end of the *saṁkrama* are the *stambhas* of the free-standing *toraṇa* at the bridge end. The *stambhas* of the gateway *toraṇa* are included with the *esikānī*.

Plate. II. Three reliefs from Sāñcī:

Fig. 4. Kapilavatthu (The Great Renunciation, see Marshall, *Guide to Sanci*, p. 60). One of the *kavāṭa* is shown half open, and behind it stands a *dovārika* (or deity acting as such), half seen. The bridge is provided with a palisade parapet like the city wall. The *toraṇa* at the bridge end is clearly shown. Buildings within the city are seen above (beyond) the city wall, on the left. By a side door women have access to the moat and are fetching water. Sāñcī, east *toraṇa*. See also Fig. A.

Fig. 5. Jettutara (*Vessantara Jātaka*, see Marshall, *Guide*, p. 53). A woman is standing in the *mukha* of the gateway, between the two *aṭṭālakas*; another carrying a *bhiṁkāra* (*Jāt*. VI, 345) stands on what would be the bridge, if bridge and moat had been shown. Buildings within the city are seen above the city wall on the right, and above (beyond) the gate-house. Sāñcī, north *toraṇa*.

Fig. 6. Kusināra (War of the Relics, see Marshall, *Guide*, p. 49). Gate-house of usual type on the left, an armed soldier standing in the *mukha* between the *aṭṭālaka*. City wall and moat, with attacking soldiers in centre. On the right a second gate of another type (see drawing, Fig. C). Within the city wall on the left, an *antaraṭṭāla*. Other buildings in the city are seen above the wall between the two gates. Sāñcī, south *toraṇa*. Cf. *Jātaka*, VI, 400 "When they were in the moat, attempting to destroy the wall, the men in the towers (*antaraṭṭālesu*) dealt havoc with arrows, javelins, spears, and so forth."

Plate. III. Mathurā and Sāñcī:

Fig. 7. (Kusinārā, War of the Relics ?), walled city with gate-house to right; the *kavāṭa* are indicated. Outside the city wall is an apsidal shrine (the only example anywhere illustrated in an old relief). Mathurā, perhaps first century A.D., I 38 in the Mathurā Museum, *Catalogue* p. 140.

Fig. 8. Kusinārā (War of the Relics, Marshall, *Guide*, p. 69). Army of the Mallas entering the city by the gate-house. Accessory defence tower (*antaraṭṭāla*) on the right. Immediately left of the gate-house, within the city, is a minor gateway of a common type. Sāñcī, west *toraṇa*.

Fig. 9. Jettutara (*Vessantara Jātaka*, Marshall, *Guide*, p. 54). Women with water jars are emerging from the *mukha* of the gate-house. Buildings within the city above (beyond) the wall and gate-house. Accessory defence tower within wall to right of gate-house (next to horse's head). The gate-house has two *harmya* storeys in place of the usual one, making four floors in all. Sāñcī, north *toraṇa*.

Fig. 10. Sāvatthi (?) (see Marshall, *Guide*, p. 59). A horseman is issuing from the *mukha*. Buildings are seen within the city above (beyond) the gate-house, on the left and city wall on the right. Sāñcī, north *toraṇa*.

Fig. 11. Rājagaha (see Marshall, *Guide*, p. 65). A chariot is emerging from the *mukha* of the gate-house. The city wall is seen as usual, to left of the gate-house (above the horses), but then turns abruptly upwards so that only the coping is visible, seen from above—an interesting and unusual consequence of the vertical projection. A building within the city is seen just above (beyond) the gate-house; and a small accessory defence tower just within the wall to the left of the gate-house. Sāñcī, east *toraṇa*.

Plate. IV. Sāñcī and Amarāvatī:

Fig. 12. Rājagaha ? (see Marshall, *Guide*, p. 60). King in chariot issuing from the *mukha* of a city gate; city wall to left. City or palace buildings within. Sāñcī, north *toraṇa*.

Fig. 13. *Chaddanta Jātaka*. Men passing in and out of a city or palace gate-house, king seated in palace within. Part of city or palace wall seen below. Amarāvatī.

Fig. 14. Cortege issuing from a city or palace gate, king seated in palace within to left. No part of the wall is seen, but the free-standing *toraṇa* in front of the gate at the bridge end is seen (or possibly this *toraṇa* belongs to a sacred enclosure to right, which the king on horseback is about to visit). Amarāvatī.

Fig. 15. Kusinārā. Partition of the Buddha's relics. A Malla chieftain with a reliquary, on an elephant, emerging from the *mukha* of the gate-house of the city. Within the city, right, above, the division of the relics, below, dancers in honour of the relics. In the foreground an accessory defence tower, not as usual within, but forming a part of the wall, of which a small part is seen extending downwards to the right. Amarāvatī, Madras Museum.

Fig. 16. King on elephant issuing from the *mukha* of a city gate; the umbrella-bearer has just passed under the free-standing *toraṇa* at the bridge end. A small part of the wall is shown immediately below and to right of the horse. Amarāvatī.

FIG. 23. MATHURĀ

FIG. 24. BHARHUT

FIG. 25. BHARHUT

Bodhi-gharas, Mathurā and Bharhut

PLATE CXXIX. *Coomaraswamy: Early Indian Architecture*

Fig. 17. Story not identified: a woman thrown over a city wall, king seated in palace above. To the right is one tower of a gate-house, the rampart extending downwards from it to the lower margin. The second tower, to right, is not preserved. Amarāvatī, Madras Museum.

Plate V. Mediæval and modern city and fortress gate-houses:

Fig. 18. Jaipur, city gate. Note the three storeys, the middle one of *harmya* type, the upper a railed roof-apartment exactly corresponding to the *uttamāgāra* of the old gate-houses.

Fig. 19. Bījāpur: bridge, gateway, and two flanking towers. Both figures after Reuther, *Indische Paläste und Wohnhauser*.

Plate VI. Mediæval and modern city and fortress gate-houses.

Fig. 20. Gateway in city wall, Dabhoi. One open gate-leaf (*kavāṭa*) is seen to left in the middle of the *śālā*, between the two double *toraṇas:* at the base of the *kavāṭa* is seen the accessory door (*aṇidvāra*, *cūḷadvāra*) for the use of pedestrians when the *kavāṭa* are closed.

Fig. 21. Gwāliar, Hāthī Paur of Mān Siṅgh's palace, ca. 1500 A.D.; showing the two side towers, and the *toraṇa* of the gate-proper (the gate being open, one leaf is seen).

II. Bodhi-gharas

In a numerous series of representations of the Bodhi tree, from Bharhut, Mathurā, and Amarāvatī, and all dateable within the four centuries ca. 175 B.C. to 225 A.D., the tree with its accessories (*vajrāsana* and a symbol) is represented as surrounded by a two- or occasionally three-storeyed hypaethral temple. Such temples of the or any Bodhi-tree are referred to in the literature as *Bodhi-gharas* (*Mahāvaṁsa*, XXXVI, 31[16] and XXXVII, 15 and 31). Strictly speaking any Bodhi-tree, with or without a temple structure, is also a *rukkha-cetiya* or *caitya-vṛkṣa*, or tree-shrine; but these terms in the Buddhist literature seem to be reserved wholly or mainly for tree-shrines not specifically Buddhist.

More or less detailed references to the manner in which a Bodhi-tree was worshipped, and to Bodhi-gharas are found in various places. In the *Aśokāvadāna*, Aśoka, having vowed to pour upon the Bodhi-tree at Bodhgayā perfumed water from four thousand precious vessels "let make an enclosure surrounding the Bodhi-tree on all four sides, and mounting upon it," fulfilled his vow.[17] It is impossible to say certainly whether by "enclosure" a permanent Bodhi-ghara is to be understood; from the Chinese words employed we can only deduce that the structure was rather of the scaffolding type, made of wood and not of stone (it is obvious that all but one of the Bodhi-gharas here discussed and illustrated were actually wooden structures).

The Sanskrit form *caturdiśaṁ vāraṁ baddhvā svāyam eva ca vāram abhiruhya caturbhiḥ kumbhasahasrair bodhisnapanaṁ kṛtavān*, corresponding exactly to the rendering from the Chinese already given, occurs in the *Divyāvadāna*, p. 404. The editors, following Burnouf, render *vāraṁ* as "platform;" but "enclosure" would be preferable. Przyluski's suggestion of "bassin" to hold the water poured at the foot of the tree is untenable, since Aśoka mounted upon it: the enclosure must have been a sort of

[16]Here *Mahābodhighare pācīne* should be rendered "on the east side of the Great Temple of the Bodhi-tree," not as by Geiger, "in the eastern temple of the Great Bodhi-tree."

[17]Przyluski, J., *La légende de l'Empereur Açoka*, 1923, pp. 267, 433.

[18]In the *Divyāvadāna* version *baddhvā*, "tied" seems at first sight to support the idea of a temporary scaffolding: but it should be remembered that this constructional method was employed even in the case of permanent wooden buildings (see IAT, p. 265, *s. v. nārāca*, and also the *Rāmāyaṇa* passage cited by Cunningham, *Stupa of Bharhut*, p. 100).

FIG. 26. VISIT OF AŚOKA AND ASSAULT OF MĀRA

FIG. 27. VISIT OF DEITIES

FIG. 28. VISIT OF ASOKA

Bodhi-gharas, Sāñcī

gallery, and may have been a finished Bodhi-ghara.[18] All the Bodhi-gharas represented in the reliefs are in the same way essentially enclosing galleries, large and strong enough to bear the weight of several persons. As in the case of temples generally, so in our case of the tree-temples, it may be safely assumed that there existed a close relation between form and function—the structure was not merely honorific, but was adapted to requirements determined by the nature of the usual offices; for the actual lustration of a tree, only a high surrounding gallery could have served.

Whether or not the "enclosure" of the *Aśokāvadāna* was a permanent Bodhi-ghara there can be little doubt that in the second century B.C. the Bodhi-tree was already surrounded by a structural Bodhi-ghara, since it is so shown in reliefs at Bharhut and Sāñcī (Figures 22, 36, etc.); these reliefs are supposed to represent the Bodhi-ghara built by Aśoka, as indeed may actually have been the case. It may be this original Bodhi-ghara which is referred to in a Bodhgayā pillar inscription as the *rājapāsāda cetikā*;[19] and that it only ceased to exist in its original form (very likely restored or rebuilt as occasion required) when it was replaced, perhaps in the time of Huviṣka, anyhow not later than in the Gupta period, by the present "Great Gandhakuṭi of the Vajrāsana.[20]" When this temple of the *vajrāsana* was built as a structure not open to the sky, the Bodhi-tree had of course to be moved, and there could have been no fundamental objection to this, since it is the position of the *vajrāsana*, rather than that of the tree, that is of cosmic significance. This new temple was built just after the time when the Buddha image had began to take its place as the principal cult object; the cult of the tree, though it has never been discontinued, thus lost its primary importance, and it is probably for this reason that the building of elaborate Bodhi-gharas seems to have ceased soon after the close of the second century, there being no representations of hypaethral temples subsequent to the late Āndhra reliefs.

The bestowing of royal consecration on a Bodhi-tree is several times mentioned in the *Mahāvaṁsa*, thus XVIII, 36, "Aśoka consecrated the Great Bodhi-tree as king of his realm." That this kind of consecration has been bestowed is perhaps to be understood whenever, as in Figures 22, 23, 26, etc. we see the tree surmounted by or provided with a *chatta* or royal umbrella.

In *Jātaka* No. 479 (*Jātaka*, IV, 229–236) the honouring of another Bodhi-tree, that planted by Ānanda at the Jetavana monastery in the Buddha's own life-time, is described in greater detail, and the ceremonies are called collectively a *Bodhi-maha*, or Festival of a Bodhi-tree. The king offers to this tree "eight hundred jars of scented water furnished with water-lilies, and a long row of full-vessels," worships the tree with music, wreaths, and cartloads of flowers, has an altar (*vajrāsana*) and a railing (*vedikā*) made of the seven precious substances, spreads golden sand in the courtyard (*aṅgana*) about the tree, and builds about the whole Wisdom-area (*Bodhi-maṇḍa*) an outer enclosing wall (*pākāra*) with a gate-house (*dvāra-koṭṭhaka*) again of the seven precious substances. Nothing is said about a Bodhi-ghara in this case.

The smoothing and sanding of the *aṅgana* or courtyard about a Bodhi-tree are also mentioned in *Mahāvaṁsa*, XXXV, 89 and XXXVI, 103; in the last place, the *vajrāsana* is spoken of as a *vedi*. In the *Mahāvaṁsa*, XLIX, 74, Aggabodhi IX has the "ruined temple (*ghara*) of the Prince of Trees newly and durably built and gilded."

A total number of eleven Bodhi-gharas is represented in the early reliefs—three at Bharhut, two at Mathurā, four at Sāñci, and two at Amarāvatī;[21] all these are reproduced on the accompanying plates. It may be that all these representations designate the original Bodhi-tree at Bodhgayā (Uruvelā of the early texts); and this may be taken for granted in most cases, though the point has little importance for present

[19]Cunningham, *Mahabodhi*, Pl. X, inscription No. 10: Bloch, *Notes on Bōdh Gayā*, A. S. I., A. R., 1908–09, p. 147. The inscription is one of those of Kuraṁgī, queen of Indrāgnimitra, and dateable about 100 B.C.

[20]Bloch, *Notes on Bōdh Gayā*, A. S. I., A. R., 1908–09, p. 153.

[21]Those from Bharhut are now in the Indian Museum, Calcutta; one from Mathurā is in the Museum of Fine Arts, Boston, the other in the Archaeological Museum, Mathurā; those at Sāñci are *in situ*; those from Amarāvati are in the Government Museum, Madras.

FIG. 29. SĀÑCĪ

FIG. 30. AMARĀVATĪ

FIG. 31. MATHURĀ

FIG. 32. AMARĀVATĪ

Bodhi-gharas, Sāñcī, Mathurā, and Amarāvati

purposes. It is not to be doubted that some of the countless memorial Bodhi-trees planted as cult objects elsewhere, like the one in Ceylon of which we have precise information in the *Mahāvaṁsa*, were provided with Bodhi-gharas; indeed, it is very probable that the whole cult and temple type of Buddhist "tree-worship" were taken over from the pre-existing and co-existing animistic practise. Even according to the Buddhist texts, the Bodhi-tree at Uruvelā was already, before the coming of the Bodhisattva, a sacred tree, the haunt of a Devatā, no doubt a Yakṣa, to whom offerings were made and from whom marriage and fertility boons might be expected. It is impossible that Buddhists should have themselves invented the details of a tree cult, which, whatever interpretation they put upon it, can easily be shown to have existed from a remote antiquity. If they were certainly not the first, for example, to hang wreaths and garlands on sacred trees, it is very possible that they were not the first to build tree-temples. Texts (cited in my *Yakṣas*, pp. 17 ff.) show that at least in many significant details, e.g. the use of umbrellas, the offering of flowers and scents, the spreading of sand, the building of enclosing walls, the honours paid to sacred trees haunted by Devatās were the same as those offered to Bodhi-trees. Moreover, the great variety of form of the Bodhi-gharas as seen in the reliefs, and the elaborate construction of even the earliest examples (Figure 22) are further proof of the antiquity of the type. The architectural style is further, in all cases, a purely Indian one, identical with that of contemporary secular building.

As already remarked, the main essentials of the special form common to all examples are determined by the nature of the case; the Bodhi-ghara is always a gallery surrounding the tree and *vajrāsana*, and necessarily open to the sky. Apparently the simplest form is represented by a cross-bar medallion relief from the Mathurā District, now in Boston (Figure 23). Here there are four outer corner pillars, and four inner pillars may be assumed, the ground plan being square. The eight pillars sloping slightly inwards, support a heavy timbered superstructure corbelled outwards, to form a flat gallery or promenade above, much wider than the basement itself; the flat surface of this aerial *padakkhiṇa* path supports no further construction: only an umbrella and banners are planted upon it. The whole structure seems to be built of a size only just sufficient to enclose the tree itself, and this seems to be confirmed by the fact that the *vajrāsana*, which has upon it three five-finger marks (*pañcaṅgulika*),[22] is seen outside and not within the structure. There is however an arched porch of the usual type, and some kind of symbol, perhaps a *ratna-traya*, is seen within; the faint suggestion of a seated Buddha figure is of course deceptive. The corbelled superstructure with its battlemented parapet belongs to an architectural type very characteristic at Bharhut (cf. Cunningham, *Stupa of Bharhut*, Pl. XXXI, 1) Bhājā (*hammiyas* of the monolithic stupas), and Sāñcī, and this fact, together with the inward slope of the pillars, suggests a date not later than the end of the second century B.C.

Of the Bharhut examples, dateable about 175 B.C., the most remarkable is that of the Prasenajit pillar, here Figure 22, with its inscription *Bhagavato Sakamunino Bodho*, "The Illumination of the Blessed Sākya-muni."

Bloch[23] supposed that this structure was supported on thirty-two pillars; Cunningham reckoned sixteen only, and drew accordingly a plan (*Mahābodhi*, Pl. II) incorporating the positions of a few pillar bases discovered in the foundations of the present Great Gandhakuṭi.

In my plan, Figure 37, the number of pillars is also taken as sixteen. The plan, on the left, is a ground plan, and shows eight of the pillars; on the right, it is a plan of the

[22]That *pañcangulika means* "hand impression" and not "palmette" as suggested in IAT., p. 267, is proved by the following passages additional to those cited in IAT.: Cull V, 18; DhA. III, 374; J. I, 166 and 193, and VI, 42; Bhāsa, *Pratimānāṭaka*, III, 11 and 38; Bana, *Harṣacarita*, 63, 13 and 157, 1. The subject is fully treated by Vogel, *The sign of the Spread Hand or "Five-finger Token" (pañcaṅgulika) in Pali literature*, K. akad. van Wetenschapen, afd. *Letterkunde*, 5e Reeks, Deel IV, Amsterdam, 1919.

[23]Bloch, Th., *Notes on Bodh-gayā*, A. S. I., A. R., 1908–09. This author quite needlessly supposes that the pillars must have been of stone.

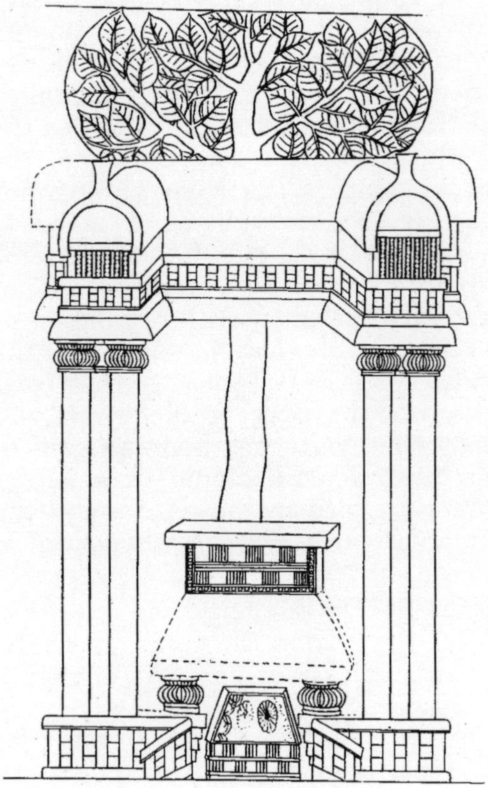

FIG. 33. DIAGRAM FROM FIG. 30

FIG. 34. RESTORATION OF FIG. 32

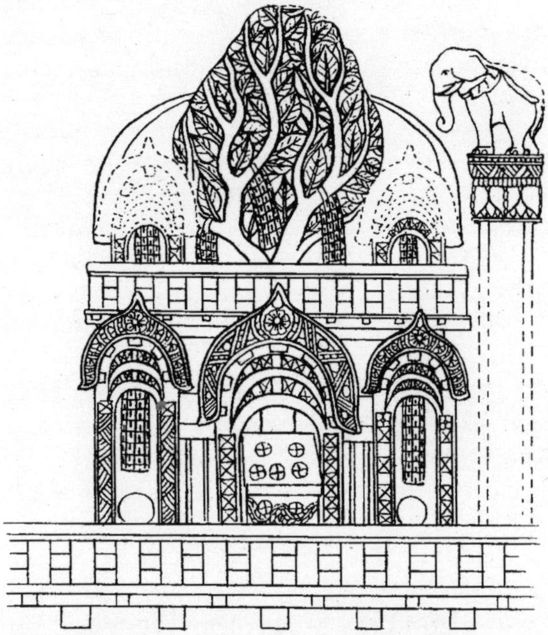

FIG. 35. DIAGRAM FROM FIG. 24

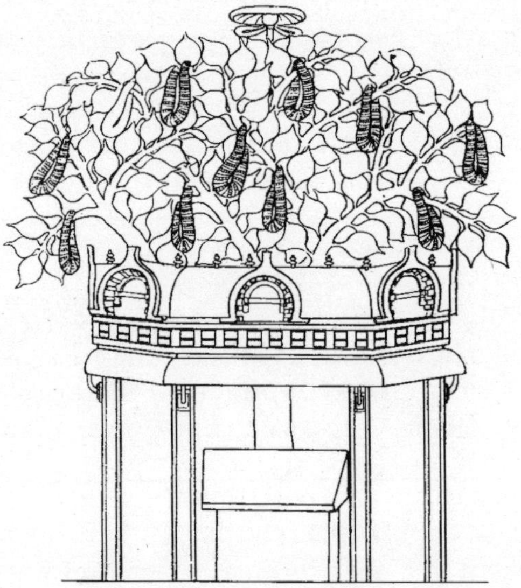

FIG. 36. DIAGRAM FROM FIG. 28

Bodhi-gharas, drawn and restored from the reliefs

PLATE CXXXII. *Coomaraswamy: Early Indian Architecture*

second storey, where we find upon a very familiar type of roof chamber or bungalow provided with numerous arched "French windows" (*mahā-vātapāna*) and a domed roof with finials. Within each window arch is seen a *chatta*. Female worshippers are seen on the balcony, between the walls of the roof chamber and the railed parapet (*vedikā*) of the gallery. Within, below, are seen the decorated trunk of the Bodhi-tree, flanked by two *ratna-traya* symbols on short pillars, and with the *vajrāsana*, supported on short columns, in front of it; the *vajrāsana* is covered with flowers, and there are four lay worshippers. It is assumed that here, as in all other cases, the *vajrāsana* is actually the central element of the plan; since it is the *vajrāsana* and not the tree which occupies the exact centre of the *Bodhi-maṇḍa* or Wisdom-area. Above, the head of the tree, decorated with wreaths and two *chattas*, rises within the circular gallery; it is worshipped, probably by two deities, and a pair of *supaṇṇas* flying towards it. Of these last, the one on the right bears a garland, the one on the left a leaf basket (*paṇṇa-pacchi* or *puṭa*) full of flowers, which he is casting one by one towards the tree. Below, on the right, external to the Bodhi-ghara, is a *dhaja-thabha* surmounted by an elephant holding a garland.

This standard example establishes the general type found elsewhere, though the plans and details vary. Another Bodhi-ghara at Bharhut, Figures 24 and 35, has evidently an apsidal plan (Figure 39), like that of the usual rock-cut *cetiva-gharas:* as before, the gallery supports a long roof chamber, but this terminates in *mahā-vātapānas* at each side, and does not continue across the front of the gallery.

As in the *cetiya-gharas* there are three entrances or porches, one central, and one corresponding to each aisle. Outside there is again a *dhaja-thabha* surmounted by an elephant.

In one other Bharhut relief, Figure 25, we have a unique case of a Bodhi-ghara seen from within; it is a square in plan, and what we see is only one of the four sides of the gallery and roof chamber with its windows, each with a projecting balcony; the courtyard (*aṅgana*) surrounding the tree and *vajrāsana*, and overlooked by the gallery, is filled with seated worshippers.[24] The central object in each of these "French windows" is a hanging garland, as also in the case of the two lateral porches.

Of the Sāñcī examples, one (Figure 28, drawn more clearly in Figure 36, and in ground and gallery plan, Figure 38) from the east *toraṇa*, lower architrave, front, forms the centre of a composition representing the visit of Aśoka, as alluded to above in a citation from the *Aśokāvadāna*. Aśoka himself is seen on the right, descending from his elephant, and followed by a queen. The structure, a little difficult to make out because of a fracture in the stone on the right side, is octagonal and supports a continuous roof chamber of the same plan and usual type. A heavy roll moulding or eaves runs round the whole structure immediately above the tops of the supporting pillars and below the gallery floor; the outer edge of these eaves is supported by brackets which spring from the pillars.

Another Sāñcī example, second panel on the left pillar, front face, of the same *toraṇa*, here Figure 27, is a type practically identical with the last, but rather more clearly represented and better preserved. Branches of the tree emerge from the outer windows of the roof chamber, and must be understood as passing also through the inner windows which are not visible.[25]

[24]Where, as in this case, the plan is square or rectangular, we have a building type exactly corresponding to that of an ordinary palace, for the term *mahāvātapana* cf. *Jātaka*, II, 21, where we have a reference to the great windows ("French windows," as I have called them here) overlooking the palace court (*rājaṅgana*).

Gavākṣa is used synonymously; so too is *sīhara-pañjara*, but here the projecting dormer as well as the actual dormer window is implied.

Architecturally and functionally these early balcony windows correspond to the modern *jharokhā*. In the *Hindī Śabda Sāgara*, *gavākṣa* is given in explanation of *jharokhā*.

Windows will be discussed more fully in a later article.

[25]Marshall, *Guide to Sanchi*, p. 65, associates with this panel the one above it, in which are seen two groups of persons separated by a horizontal band. In my opinion these are not deities looking on at the Illumination represented below. More probably (as suggested in Sir John Marshall's footnote) the upper panel represents the Great Miracle at Śrāvastī, and in this case the horizontal band must be the Buddha's *caṅkama*.

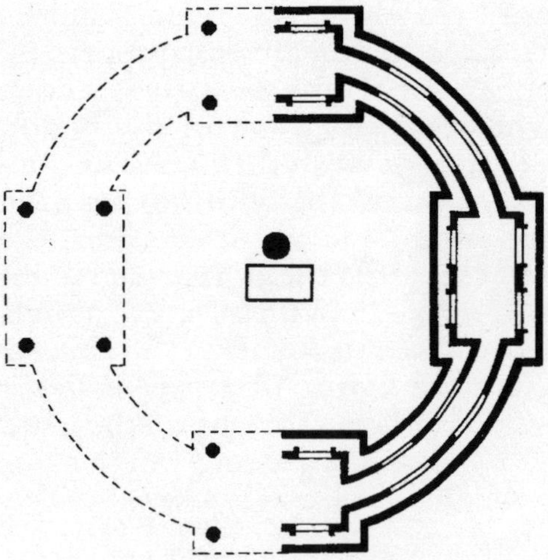

FIG. 37. PLAN OF FIG. 22

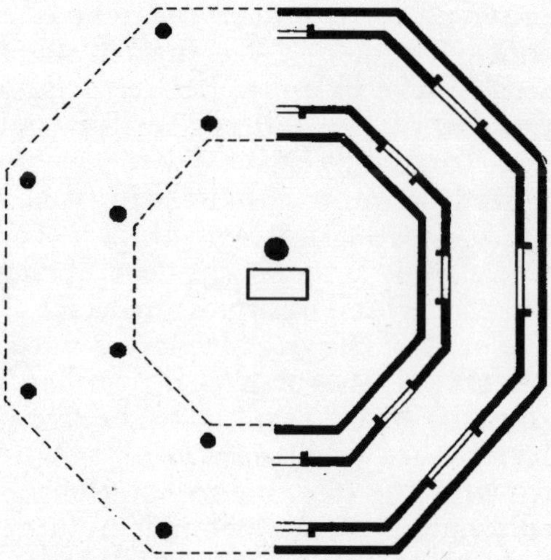

FIG. 38. PLAN OF FIGS. 28, 36

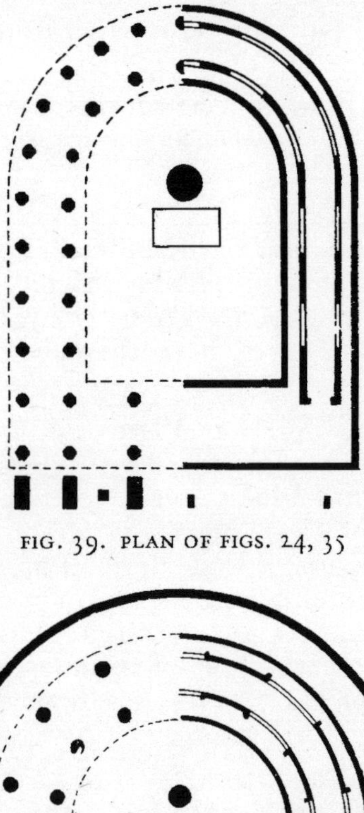

FIG. 39. PLAN OF FIGS. 24, 35

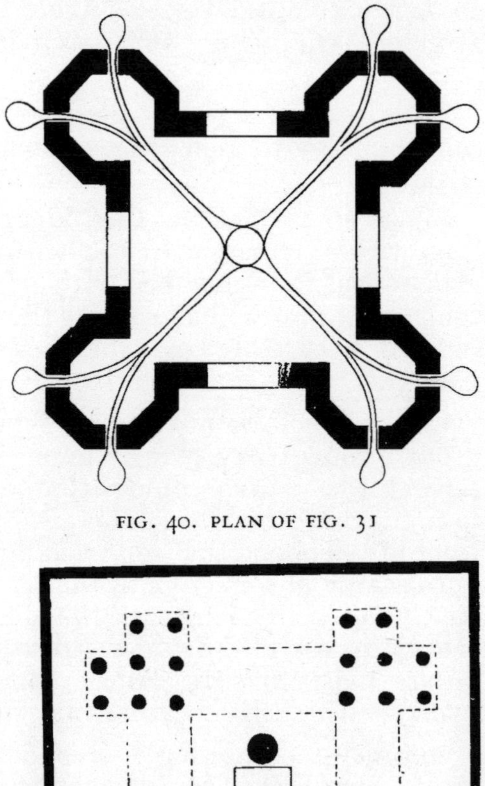

FIG. 40. PLAN OF FIG. 31

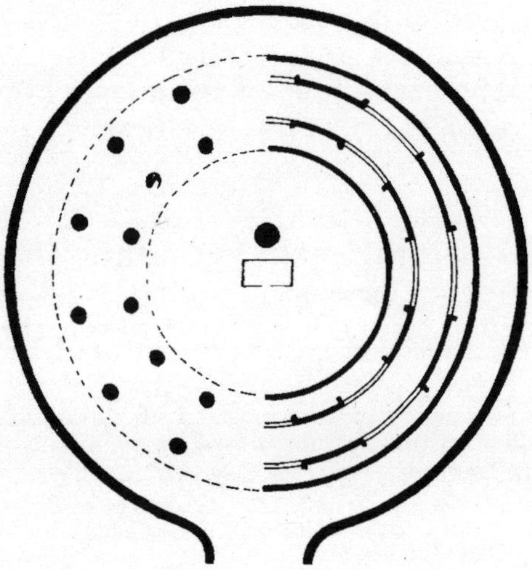

FIG. 41. PLAN OF FIG. 34

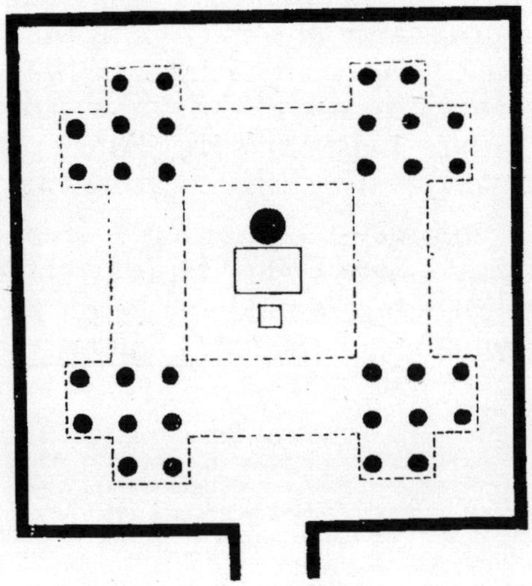

FIG. 42. PLAN OF FIGS. 30, 33

Bodhi-ghara plans

PLATE CXXXIII. *Coomaraswamy: Early Indian Architecture*

A third Sāñcī Bodhi-ghara, on the south *toraṇa*, left pillar, inner face, upper panel, here Figure 29, is an imposing circular structure, the gallery chamber having twelve windows, arranged in groups of three. The figures in the panel immediately below this may be those of Aśoka, two queens, and attendants.

The last Sāñcī example, from the west *toraṇa*, lower architrave, back, here Figure 26, is the most elaborate type anywhere represented. The scene combines, on the right, the Assault of Māra, and on the left the deities celebrating the Buddha's final victory. As remarked by Sir John Marshall, *Guide to Sanchi*, p. 69, the representation of Aśoka's Bodhi-ghara surrounding the tree is therefore in a sense an anachronism; perhaps it would be better to say that in this scene, three or even four separate events are combined, viz. the Assault of Māra, the visit of the deities, the Illumination, and the erection of Aśoka's temple. The latter is four-storeyed (three storeys besides the ground level); the uppermost storey is of the usual type, but as in the case of Figure 24 the uppermost gallery chamber ends in arched "French windows" at each side, and does not continue across the front, it must be assumed that the plan is apsidal. The two intermediate storeys are of open pillared construction, the lower only being provided with balcony windows. The ground plan would be not unlike that represented in Figure 39.

Of the two Amarāvatī examples, only one (Figure 30) is intact, and though poorly preserved can be readily interpreted (Figures 33, 42).[26] Here the gallery seems to be at an unusual height above the ground. It may be remarked that in no case is any means of access to the upper storeys indicated in the reliefs, but it is quite certain that the upper storeys were accessible (cf. the figures shown on the upper storey in Figure 22), and probable that they were used for circumambulation, though this could also have been done on the ground floor. It is perhaps worth while pointing out in this connection the parallel case of the secular *pāsāda*, mansion or palace, where the inhabited rooms are always on the second or other upper floor, and access is by means of a stair (e.g. J., III, 216, *sopāna*, and 239, *pāsādam abhirūhi*, etc.); in the representations of *pāsādas* we see persons on the upper storey balconies, but the stairway is never shown, as it would not be visible in an exterior view.

The second Amarāvatī example is a mere fragment (Figure 32), but what remains is well preserved and lends itself to a fairly complete restoration (Figure 34). The structure was evidently circular, with two storeys above the ground level. The tentative plan, Figure 41, cannot be very far removed from what would be inferable also in the case of the Sāñcī temple of Figure 29.

There remains one Bodhi-ghara (Figure 31) of unique form, occurring in a panel of an architrave from Mathurā, probably of early second century. This is evidently a walled structure; in the plan (Figure 40), drawn at the level of the lower protruding branches of the tree, it is assumed that there were doors on all four sides, but this may not have been the case, for this is evidently a protective, and not merely an honorific structure. The building seems to have been square, with octagonal corner towers; no other form satisfactorily explains the relief.

All known representations of Bodhi-gharas have now been illustrated and more or less successfully interpreted. The type is a very special one, and with all its variations of detail, of great interest; it occupies a logical place in a stylistically unified architectural tradition, and the present attempts at interpretation, together with such revisions and corrections as may be made later, must certainly throw some light on the building methods in general, as will appear when the secular domestic and palace architecture are subsequently discussed.

[26]For a discussion of the scene in which this representation appears see Rūpam, 38, 39, pp. 72, 73.

Plate VII.

Fig. 22. Circular *Bodhi-ghara* (see plan, Fig. 37). The whole represents the Great Enlightenment (inscription on the roof, *Bhagavato Saka-munino bodho*). Notice the umbrellas and garlands on the Bodhi-tree; umbrellas with garlands seen through the *mahāvātapāna* openings on the gallery level, and female figures standing on the gallery verandah; above, Supaṇṇas bringing flowers and garlands, and standing worshipping Devas, and below, lay worshippers, male and female; two *ratna-traya* symbols behind the altar, between them the decorated trunk of the Bodhi-tree; flower-offerings on the *vajrāsana*. Apparently two *tala* palms (omitted in the plan) are enclosed by the Bodhi-ghara, one on each side of the Bodhi-tree. The connected scenes below represent the Devas assembled in worship, Māra grieving at his defeat, etc. On the right, external to the Bodhi-ghara, and extending downward into the scene below, is a *dhaja-thabha* with an elephant capital (not shown in the plan). Bharhut, ca. 150–175 B.C. Indian Museum, Calcutta.

Plate VIII.

Fig. 23. Square *Bodhi-ghara*, with heavy corbelled roof-gallery. Umbrella and two banners on upper level, two banners at side; altar in front with *pañcangulikāni*. From a railing cross-bar medallion, Mathurā, second century B.C., Museum of Fine Arts, Boston.

Fig. 24. Apsidal *Bodhi-ghara* (see diagram, Fig. 35 and plan, Fig. 39), situated in a grove of similar trees. The three porches open into the nave and two aisles of the whole structure, which must have resembled in plan the ordinary rock-cut *cetiya-gharas* or caitya-halls. Through the central porch opening are seen the *vajrāsana* and trunk of the Bodhi-tree. On the right is a *dhaja-thabha* with an elephant capital. Four lay worshippers, or perhaps the Four Regents or Mahārājas. Bharhut, 150–175 B.C. Indian Museum, Calcutta.

Fig. 25. Interior court (*angana*) of a square *Bodhi-ghara*, showing, above, the inner side of the gallery (the two side pillars and architrave with battlement and lotus motifs are not a part of the scene). In the centre of the court are the Bodhi-tree, and *vajrāsana* with an umbrella. Two Supaṇṇas are bringing flower offerings in *paṇṇa-pacchis*, and casting them toward the tree (an act of worship). In the courtyard, round the tree, are seated twenty-seven male persons, probably Devas. Bharhut, as before.

Plate IX.

Fig. 26. Apsidal *Bodhi-ghara* with three upper storeys. To the right, the Assault of Māra, to the left, Visit of the Devas, the whole scene representing the Great Enlightenment (cf. Marshall, *Guide to Sanchi*, p. 69). Sāñcī, west *toraṇa*, in situ, ca. 50–75 B.C.

Fig. 27. Octagonal *Bodhi-ghara* (cf. plan Fig. 38), situated in a grove of mango and other fruit trees. Cf. Marshall, *Guide*, p. 65. Sāñcī, east *toraṇa*, in situ, ca. 75–100 B.C.

Fig. 28. Octagonal *Bodhi-ghara* (see diagram, Fig. 36, and plan, Fig. 38). Supaṇṇas with offerings above, worshipping Devas, perhaps the Four Regents, below. *Ratna-traya* symbol on the *vajrāsana*. Cf. Marshall, *Guide*, p. 61. Sāñcī, east *toraṇa*, lower architrave, in situ, ca. 75–100 B.C.

Plate X.

Fig. 29. Circular *Bodhi-ghara*. Three *ratna-traya* symbols on the *vajrāsana*. Cf. Marshall, *Guide*, pp. 50, 51. Sāñcī, south *toraṇa*, left pillar, in situ, ca. 100 B.C.

Fig. 30. Square *Bodhi-ghara* (see diagram, Fig. 33, and plan, Fig. 42), with tall slender pillars. Amarāvatī, ca. 200 A.D. Madras Museum.

Fig. 31. Square, walled, *Bodhi-ghara* (see plan, Fig. 40). Visit of Aśoka? From a Kusāna architrave, Mathurā, ca. 100–150 A.D. M-3 in the Mathurā Museum.

Fig. 32. Fragment of a circular *Bodhi-ghara* (see restoration Fig. 34, and plan, Fig. 41). Amarāvatī, first (?) century A.D. Madras Museum.

Plate XI.

Figs. 33–36. Diagrams of *Bodhi-gharas*, in part restored.

Plate XII.

Figs. 37–42. Plans of *Bodhi-gharas*, deduced from the reliefs.

THE LIBERAL POLITICS OF ADOLF HITLER

JOHN KING is the author of seven previous novels – *The Football Factory*, *Headhunters*, *England Away*, *Human Punk*, *White Trash*, *The Prison House* and *Skinheads*. *The Football Factory* was turned into a film in 2004 and his books have been widely translated abroad. He has written short stories and articles for a number of publications, edits the fiction fanzine *Verbal*, and is currently finishing a new novel, *Slaughterhouse Prayer*. He lives in London.